EVERY DAY, CHEMISTRY

For the Sooybeans: Henry, Teddy,
Isabelle, and Richard
—J.S.

To my dad, who was my personal tutor
for science subjects in high school
—B.P.

A FEIWEL AND FRIENDS BOOK
An imprint of Macmillan Publishing Group, LLC
120 Broadway, New York, NY 10271
mackids.com

Library of Congress Cataloging-in-Publication Data is available.

First edition, 2021
Book design by Mike Burroughs
Artwork is created digitally
Printed in China by RR Donnelley Asia Printing Solutions Ltd.,
Dongguan City, Guangdong Province
Feiwel and Friends logo designed by Filomena Tuosto

ISBN: 978-1-250-76869-8
10 9 8 7 6 5 4 3 2 1

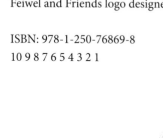

EVERY DAY, CHEMISTRY

Julia Sooy

Illustrated by Bonnie Pang

Feiwel and Friends

New York

Science is all around us.

Our bread toasting,
Our tongues tasting—

chemical reactions happen every day.

Substances become something new—not just by cutting or freezing or physical change, but by changing what they *are*, their chemical composition.

When we go for a drive
and turn the key, sparking the
engine, fuel and oxygen become
energy and exhaust.
We're chemistry in motion!

At the park, plants are growing and making food from sunshine, water, and carbon dioxide.

That's chemistry, too.

Whether we're lazing, cloud-watching with slow deep breaths, or sprinting, panting—

our respiration is chemistry.

At the playground,
the slide is rusting.

Chemical reactions transform.

Our tummies digesting,
a half-eaten apple turning brown—

that's picnic chemistry.

At bath time, shampoo foams,
lifting away sweat and dirt—
tiny chemical reactions get
our hair clean.

Our dough rising,
the stove lighting—

chemical reactions happen
in the kitchen, too.

Dishwashing liquid sudsing,
washing away oil—

it's cleanup chemistry.

The flashlight shining—
battery power!

You hold chemical
reactions in your hand.

You and me, loving—
that's chemistry, too.

Everyday chemistry.

Chemical reactions are all around!

We think of chemistry as science that happens in a laboratory. But chemical reactions happen every day—not just in labs, but in our lives.

Chemical reactions involve the transformation of substances by changing their composition—what they *are* in terms of atoms and molecules, and the bonds between them.

Ask these three questions to help determine if a chemical reaction has occurred:

1) **Did the change create something new?**

2) **Can it be easily undone or reversed?**

3) **Are there new physical properties?**

Look for changes in color or smell, or the production of heat, light, sound, or gas.

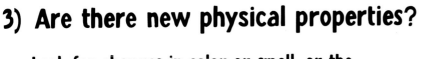

BREAD: chemical and physical changes

Chemical reactions happen in many places, but some of the most fun and easiest to observe—not to mention most delicious!—happen in the kitchen.

Consider baking bread: When you mix flour, water, yeast, and salt into dough, it starts as a small blob in the bowl. After a few hours at room temperature, what do you see?

The dough is much bigger. It is filled with air bubbles. It smells different from the ingredients you started with. A chemical reaction has occurred!

The yeast has fed on the sugar that makes up flour and produced carbon dioxide (CO_2) and another substance called ethanol.

Then, when you put the dough in a nice hot oven, how does it change?

With time it grows even bigger, becomes darker in color, and tougher in texture. It holds its shape. When you thump the loaf, it sounds hollow, not solid. Physical changes have occurred—the water in the wet dough has evaporated—but also, a chemical reaction has taken place! The sugars in the flour have caramelized.

Now, when you cut a slice of bread, it looks different from the whole loaf—but that's a physical change. The bread that makes up the loaf is the same as the bread that makes up the slice. If you toast that slice and it gets brown and crunchy (and maybe a little burnt)—that's a chemical change. The toasted bread is a different substance than the untoasted bread.

Science is delicious!